T0145152

GEORGE RAPITIS

George Michael

The Singing Greek

(A Tribute)

AuthorHouse™
1663 Liberty Drive
Bloomington, IN 47403
www.authorhouse.com
Phone: 833-262-8899

This book is printed on acid-free paper.

ISBN: 978-1-6655-3133-7 (sc)
978-1-6655-3134-4 (e)

Print information available on the last page.

Published by AuthorHouse 07/09/2021

authorHOUSE®

George Michael

The Singing Greek

(A Tribute)

Contents

Foreword

It was the 1980s, (the must tubular decade ever) we had just moved into my new neighborhood in Livonia. I was the new kid on the block and attended Emerson Jr. high school. One of my best memories was the 1984 Detroit Tigers winning the World series (Bless You Boys!). I had by chance rode my bike to Wonderland Mall to play my favorite video games and eat at the Greek restaurant in the food court. That day they just happened to have some the World Series Detroit Tigers there in to be congratulated for their huge win. Their manager Sparky Anderson, walked right passed me while I was watched by my surprise! That was the legend Sparky Anderson I thought to myself! As I grew up, I attended Livonia Franklin High School the home of the Patriots! I remember many of us wore parachute pants with high tops and watched breakdancing in the hallway between classes. Many had the big hair and the guys and girls had brightly colored fashion styles. When we got home from school we would play games on our Atari especially Pac-man and Donkey Kong or watch music videos on Mtv! (We want our Mtv!). The 80s music was totally awesome with the likes of Culture Club, Duran Duran and the Police (I once won tickets to see Sting in concert at the Franklin All night graduation party). We would have school dances that played our favorite artists which I never missed. Careless Whisper by George Michael was played at my prom! I still remember slow dancing with my date to that song at the dance! The dances were my favorite part of school along with foods and culinary arts class. After school, I would deliver papers for the Detroit News also and while I was delivering I would wear my Sony Walkman and listen to my favorite tunes on cassette tape. My mom, Koula(Carol) and sister Maria loved listening to Wham! and danced in the living room to them every evening because they were so upbeat. My brother Markos, was also a fan and enjoyed watching them too! On the weekends, I had a job at Burger King working the drive thru in order to afford to buy all my favorite cassettes. That's kind of where it all started when one of my co workers said I reminded her of a pop star George Michael. I didn't at the time know much of who he was but kind of ignored it at first. As time went on and she mentioned it more I became a fan too! I was fortunate enough to see George Michael in concert during the Cover to Cover tour and later during the 25 live tour. Now so many years later, I am still a fan and love relive the 80s the best decade because was the glue of music bringing all the decades together! I also have a totally awesome collection of George Michael memorabilia and many handmade things like jackets and vests that you will see in throughout this book to make it more unique.

It was my honor to write this book about George Michael "The Singing Greek!"

Chapter 1

The Heart of the Singing Greek

He was known to the music world as Pop Star, George Michael, however his birth name was Georgios Kyriacos Panayiotou (it doesn't get any more Greek then that!) and was born on 25 June 1963 in East Finchley, London. George Michael went on to refer to himself as the "Singing Greek" on Twitter. (***Lots of love, The Singing Greek xxx— George Michael (@GeorgeMichael)***)

The father of the "Singing Greek", Kyriacos Panayiotou, also known as "Jack" was a Greek Cypriot restaurant owner who departed for England for a better life in the 1950s. Young George (his nickname was Yog which was short for Yorgos in Greek) would spend hours working at his dad's restaurant as a teen and was very close to his sisters Melanie and Yiota.

His mother was his heart

"The Singing Greek" was especially close with his mother Leslie. George Michael loved his mom Lesley Angold Panayiotou immensely, who died in February 1997 from cancer, with all his heart. Many say that he never quite got over her passing. In his own words, George went on to say that he became interested in singing when he was seven when his Mum had given him a tape recorder as a gift. As George grew, his father was against the idea of him growing up to be a rock star but Mum began to realize that he might have special talent and started to feel he had a future in singing.

His heart gave out on Christmas Day

"Once bitten and twice shy, I keep my distance but you still catch my eye."
The Singing Greek wrote those lyrics for a song called Last Christmas, ironically pop star George Michael, died on Christmas day in 2016 at the age of 53. Later his sister, Melanie ironically also died on Christmas day 3 years to the day. He was remembered for his sex appeal, his beautiful songwriting and his amazing voice — and for his personal life, which was treated as tabloid material at times. It was the early hours of Christmas Day morning, George died at his home in Goring-on-Thames. A post-mortem report read that his death was due to natural causes. Christmas will never be the same however, he will be remembered for giving from his heart so that others can have a good Christmas through charity.

George's Pets were Members of the Family

George loved his pets especially yellow Labradors. He could be seen walking them daily and playing with them in his yard, in the village of Goring, Oxfordshire, where he had lived for 17 years. Unfortunately, his beloved pet dog Abby has died at the age of 15. The yellow Labrador was George's last surviving pet, and fans have been left saddened by the passing of his loyal pooch. The unfortunate news was shared by George's cousin Alex Georgiou, who confirmed to Heart FM that it was true.

He gave Big with his heart but wanted few to know it

While he had some big hits which were very public, he had some other hits that were not so public, you see, not everything he did was known all his fans. For example, the proceeds from the 1996 song hit "Jesus to a Child", went to a charity called ChildLine. The founder of the organization had stated that Michael had donated millions of dollars over the years, and was very strict about not giving his name so that no one outside the charity knew how much he had given. Another example of his generosity was in December 2008, Michael released a Christmas song called "December Song" on his website for free as a gift to his fans. This was followed by "True Faith « (which was a UK top 30 and Irish top 40 hit, a wonderful cover of a New Order song); and «You and I», another charity single and a gift to Prince Harry and Kate for their wedding. It was a Stevie Wonder song originally.

In addition, Michael frequently gave live music performances to support charities. One example was a free concert for nurses in the U.K. after his mother passed, saying he realized how hard nurses worked and deserved something special and wanted to thank them for their work. And what about when he was part of the 80s star cast of the Band Aid charity song "Do They Know It's Christmas?"

The executive producer of the game show *Deal or No Deal,* went on to reveal that the "Singing Greek" with a giving heart, once freely gave 15,000 pounds for a contestant who said she needed funds for IVF treatment and he did this anonymously.

In another instance, it was said he gave a woman he never met, in a cafe £25k as he overheard her weeping over a great deal of debt she was experiencing. The "Singing Greek" freely wrote a check and gave it to the waitress to give to her after he left in order to stay anonymous and avoid getting credit.

He not only gave funds but of his time because he also would volunteer at a homeless shelter and asked the workers to keep it under their hats that he was there.

Chapter 2

His Heart was in the Right Place for his idol Freddie Mercury

Dressed in a red blazer, black shirt and slacks, wearing his signature shades, George Michael was one of the performers at the Freddie Mercury Tribute Concert. This amazing night, the "Singing Greek's" heart was at Wembley Stadium in April 1992. George sang the Queen hit, 'Somebody to Love' with the rest of Queen as a tribute to the late Freddie Mercury. How appropriate as his heart was always looking to help somebody that was in need in some way!

"Somebody to Love", George stated was the most difficult song he had ever sung to a live audience in his life, but he sure did belt it out from deep within his heart. The result was an incredible performance that even invoked complete audience participation. As the George sang

"Somebody toooooo"…..the audience replied "looooooooooove"!! George would reply in approval with a " Yeaaaaaah!!"

There is even a video of him rehearsing for it backed by Queen which is available on YouTube in which he channels the late great Freddie Mercury with an incredible amount of courage and manages to belt out the vocally incredible song, with the late David Bowie and Seal as his private audience applauding.

"It's ridiculous," Michael said of the song, "one minute it's up here, one minute it's down there…" As for getting to sing it live: "It was the proudest moment of my career, but mixed with real sadness," he goes on to state in an interview.

When Michael eventually sang 'Somebody To Love' in front of thousands, the band Queen were astonished at how amazing his performance was and how much the crowd responded to him.

In 1993, the "Singing Greek" yet again with his heart alive with giving, released the *Five Live* EP, which contained tracks performed at The Freddie Mercury Tribute Concert with Queen and Lisa Stansfield. This was the album he had discussed as a charity album that he recorded for the Mercury Phoenix Trust, which was an AIDS-fighting organization dedicated to Freddie Mercury's memory.

Below are some of the charities that George Michael contributed too:

Children with AIDS
Comic Relief
Crusaid
Elton John AIDS Foundation
Goss-Michael Foundation
Gray Cancer Institute
Help a London Child
Jubilee Action
Macmillan Cancer Support
Marie Curie
Meals On Wheels
Mercury Phoenix Trust
Nottinghamshire Bereavement Trust
Outcome
Outline
Positive Nation
Project Angel Food
Rainbow Trust
Red Cross
Red Hot Organization
Rhys Daniels Trust
Sightsavers International
St John's Hospice
Swan Lifeline
Terrence Higgins Trust
The Food Chain
UK Thalassaemia Society
War Child

Chapter 3

Wham bam the Heartbeat Began!

You might wonder how did the heartbeat of Wham begin? George Michael and Andrew Ridgeley the heart and soul of Wham! became friends at Bushy Meads School in Bushey near the town of Watford in Hertfordshire. The two played concerts in a short-lived ska band called the Executive, alongside former school friend David Austin. When this group broke up, Michael and Andrew Ridgeley eventually formed Wham!

Andrew Ridgeley shared that the name came to be from a need for "something that captured the essence of what made us stand out which was our energy and our friendship and then suddenly there it was ….Wham!" The band's music was very catchy, fun and exciting too. British graphic design studio Stylorouge came up with the idea of placing the exclamation mark to the name at the end.

Ridgeley and Michael worked night and day to get their feet in the door with recording executives. In February 1982, they finally got their chance! In the early years, they would write songs such as "Wham Rap (Enjoy What You Do)" and "Club Tropicana" as a team, but during the recording of their debut album *Fantastic*, George did most of the songs.

As teens, they were portrayed as living free of work or commitment. Their early songs proved it when you listen to them, for a time this earned Wham! a reputation as a dance protest group.

"Wham Rap! was the first record that that came out in June 1982. The record had two different versions of the song. The song only made it to No. 105 unfortunately.

"Young Guns (Go for It)" came out next. At the start, it also didn't do well on the charts but the band got lucky when the popular British program *Top of the Pops* scheduled them after another act cancelled at the last minute. During their performance, George sang the vocals while Andrew Ridgeley, portrayed the part of the teenage bridegroom-in-waiting. They were joined by backing singers Dee C Lee and Shirlie Holliman.

Wham! was Everything Fans Wanted !

Fantastic (1983) and *Make It Big* (1984), had both attained number one status on the UK Albums Chart and the US *Billboard* 200. Some of the smash hits were "Wake Me Up Before You Go-Go" and "Last Christmas". These smashes propelled them into becoming a household name which led to, Wham!'s tour of China in April 1985. It was the first trip to China by a Western popular music group, and gained worldwide media attention!

To the Heart and Mind

By the end of 1983, Wham! had tough competition with bands such Culture Club and Duran Duran trying to be Britain's biggest pop acts. Their debut album *Fantastic* spent two weeks at No. 1 in the UK album charts in 1983, but the album only had modest success in the US however, that all changed with all their many hit songs that were to come. One song in particular put them apart from the rest! In fact, this song was Michael's first solo single "Careless Whisper" topped the charts to number one in over 20 countries, including the UK and US. In August 1984, it entered the UK Singles Chart at number 12 and in two weeks it shot to number one. The video for the song, is about a guilty cheater in a relationship. George is torn between two lovers and sings "please staaaay" at one point in the song. It had a deeper feel than other songs they had released in the past. At the end of the video, George stands at the top of a hotel balcony in Miami with a beautiful sunset in the background contemplating with his heart and looking into the horizon. The song would reach No. 1, selling over 1.3 million copies in the UK. "Careless Whisper" marked a new phase in Michael's career, as his label Columbia/Epic began to somewhat distance him from the group Wham!'s playboy image. Fast forward to 2021 and it recently hit over 4 Billion global streams! It has stood the test of time!

Fun Facts about the Careless Whisper Song and Video:

It was filmed on location in Miami, Florida, in February 1984
Filmed at Coconut Grove and Watson Island.
The final part depicts Michael leaning out of a top floor balcony of Miami's Grove Towers.
He was 17 when he wrote the song
It was written on a bus ride on the way to his job as an usher at the movie theater.

Wham fans hearts doing the:

Jitterbug
Jitterbug
Jitterbug
Jitterbug

It was the big 80s and a fun time to be alive. Wham! was just beginning to be heard all over the airwaves. By now you would think Andrew Ridgley would be living in a big mansion however, the interesting thing was that he actually still lived at home with his family even after Wham! could be heard all over the radio, which may sound funny. Since they were touring all the time, it was just convenient to live at home with mum. One day, Ridgeley needed a wake-up call, so he jotted a note to his mum. He wrote, "Wake me up up," and realizing he duplicated a word, finished the sentence with "before you go go."

George Michael happened to read it and was very amused with the funny note Andrew had written, and decided to use it as a title for a song and the rest is pop history! "Wake Me Up Before You Go Go," became Wham's first American hit. It became their first US and UK No. 1 single, and was paired with a video of the duo with backup singers Pepsi and Shirlie, all wearing T-shirts with the slogans "CHOOSE LIFE" and "GO GO".

Wham! Wakes China up before they Go Go

In 1985, Wham! made a historical 10-day visit to China, the first by a Western pop group! The concert was seen as an amazing moment in time which made increasing friendly international relations between China and the West. Many of the highlights can be seen in the music video Freedom by Wham!

Live Aid (1985)

Appearing in a trendy 80s beard, Michael was seen with Ridgeley onstage at Live Aid on 13 July 1985 (surprisingly they did not sing as Wham!). Michael sang "Don't Let the Sun Go Down on Me" with Elton John, while Ridgeley sang with Kiki Dee in the row of backing singers. In September, Wham! did it right and released the single "I'm Your Man" which went to No. 1 in the UK charts.

Wham! Breaks our Hearts

After much success, in 1986, Wham! called it a quits. Michael was determined to write music meant for a more sophisticated audience rather than the duo's teen crowd. Soon after the breakup of Wham! Before going in different directions, a final single "The Edge of Heaven", and a greatest hits album titled *The Final* would be available as well a last concert called *The Final*. The last single scored a No. 1 hit June 1986. "Where Did Your Heart Go?" was the group's final single in the United States. This London duo had been a music team for five years, selling over 28 million records and 15 million singles. *Foreign Skies*, their tour which took place in China, received its world premiere at the Final Concert.

Wham Fans broken Hearts Go to Wembley

Saturday, 28 June 1986, London's Wembley Stadium is where Wham! said so long to their fans and each other with an touching embrace at the end of its final concert. Over 72,000 fans were there for the eight-hour concert, which included support artists such as Elton John! It was an extremely hot day but that didn't stop everyone from having a magical night.

"Everything She Wants" was the introduction track after 8 minutes and began from behind a giant black curtain which read "The Final" on it in huge white letters. It opened to reveal Michael donned in leather, black jeans, wearing sunglasses and dancing at the same time with two other dancers. Ridgeley, Shirley and Pepsi entered the stage. Ridgeley removed his black coat and strutted up the walkways and then removed his black gloves. The Wham hit "Club Tropicana" followed. Michael then spoke into the microphone to the audience to tell them "This is the best thing I've ever looked at". We've got four years of thank-yous to say this evening... and I know we're going to enjoy saying them. So let's get started!". The songs "Heartbeat" and "Battlestations" were played next and the celebration continued!!

What happened to Andrew Ridgely?

It's a question that comes up quite often! Soon after they went their separate ways, Andrew decided to relocate to Monaco, and drive Formula Three motor racing. He then went on to relocate to Los Angeles for a career in acting as well and release a cd called "Son of Albert." However, he returned to the UK in 1990 and settled there. Andrew, writing in his best selling autobiography, confirmed it was a mutual break-up, and had nothing but love for his late friend.

Chapter 4

You Gotta have Faith in the Sound When You go Solo!

George Michael was now going solo and had to compete with the likes of Prince and Madonna. It wouldn't be an easy task; however, his solo album would do just that! The Album *Faith*, by George Michael came out in 1987, heading right to the top of the UK Albums Chart and placing number one on the *Billboard* 200 for 12 weeks. In fact, at the MTV awards, Madonna would present him with a Lifetime Achievement Award where he kissed the Queen of Pop back in 1989. She would go on to announce: "The award goes to George Michael!!!"

The entire Faith album is amazing and will always be a classic. Every song could have been a single however, the main singles are below.

The Four singles from the album that hit number one were:
"Faith"
"Father Figure"
"One More Try"
"Monkey"
"Kissing a Fool" ***

All reached number one on the *Billboard* Hot 100 and had very memorable videos.

Here are some more fun facts about FAITH:
Faith was awarded Album of the Year at the 1989 Grammy Awards.
The album peaked at number one in the UK Albums Chart, and was certified 4× Platinum by the British Phonographic Industry (BPI).
It also peaked at number one on the US *Billboard* 200 and was certified Diamond for sales of over 10 million copies.

But I Gotta think twice before I give my heart away

The Singing Greek goes solo and the result is the FAITH video where he wears a sleek black leather jacket with the letters BSA on the back, tight denim-clad ripped jeans and shaking his butt just-so to an infectious beat.

Fun facts about this video:

The BSA leather jacket was just purchased the night before with his sister.

The leather jacket was bought in Leathers and Treasures on LA's Melrose Avenue.

The old Gretsch guitar he plays was found in a pawn shop.

He didn't actually know how to play the guitar.

Put it all together and the rest is 80s Pop music video history!!

George Michael put his heart into his hits especially these!

'Faith'
'Careless Whisper'
'One More Try'
'Wake Me Up Before You Go-Go'
'Everything She Wants'
'Freedom 90'

Below are some of the Faith Album Fan favorite lyrics:

"I've had enough of danger and people on the streets. I'm looking out for angels, just trying to find some peace."
One More Try

"People, you can never change the way they feel, better let them do just what they will."
Kissing A Fool

Well I guess it would be nice, if I could touch your body. I know not everybody, has got a body like you."
Faith

Aretha Franklin and George sing their hearts out to Number 1!

One of the most memorable nights during the "Faith World Tour", took place on Aug. 30, 1988. Motown legend, Aretha Franklin, joined George Michael on stage in Auburn Hills, Michigan. Together they sang their smash duet "I knew you were waiting" which was a number one hit, to a packed house at the Palace of Auburn hills for over 24,000 fans! It won the 1987 Grammy award for best R&B performance by a Duo or Group with vocal for that song. Aretha Franklin, the queen of soul, fondly remembered how friendly and personable George was while filming the music video for the song. The video and song were both completed in Detroit. So, when they sang it together in Detroit it made it even more special! Even now over 34 years later, it sounds even better! "I still believe!!"

A Taste of the FAITH Tour

Speaking of believing, night after night during the FAITH tour, George Michael wowed shrieks of swooning fans. while wearing his signature "dangling earrings" which were his trademark at the time.

He would burn through a 14-song set -- plus two encore songs -- stuffed with hits from his then-new album, "Faith", songs from the disbanded duo Wham! that propelled him to fame, and bouncy covers from megastars like Stevie Wonder.

When George Michael was on stage, he would use his charismatic stage presence to induce universal swoons among teenaged girls and sometimes their mothers as well. After the song "Hard Day" he would ask them "Do you trust me?" meaning do you trust me that you will have a fun time (Yea!) He was at the height of his powers, on the Faith tour. During the infectious dance grooves, he would include a several well-placed dance bumps, a few grunts enough to bring teeny bopper squeals to the point that it would bring the stadium roof to the ground. In addition, sometimes he was bare-chested under his sleek leather jacket and looked dazzling while wearing a dangling cross earring. Michael wowed fans who would travel from all across the cities like they were on a pilgrimage, many of them decked out in their favorite 1980s attire such as bold colors, and silhouettes—big permed hair. Others dressed in ripped tights and biker jackets, polished baggy blazers and girls wearing poof skirts.

Fans of all ages came to see this man with the carefully highlighted hair and tight clad jeans, who sings of love and safe sex, with so much magnetism!

Beyond his amazing charisma, his songs were based around calls for love. It was an amazing period in Michael›s career, as the then-25-year-old singer so well loved by his fans, had not yet disclosed his personal love preferences. During this tour he offered up songs like "Faith" that calls for true devotion alongside the song that pushes the envelope the infamous "I Want Your Sex." All in the new, fresh on the scene age of MTV and Vh1. However, at the end of the tour his heart felt there needed to be something more….

Chapter 5

Listen with Your Heart: The Post FAITH Years

When it was time to do his next album, George felt it was time for fans to listen more with their hearts then their eyes. The Singing Greek wanted the new album to have a deeper meaning so he named his next, album "Listen Without Prejudice Vol. 1" it was instantly a UK number-one and included the Billboard Hot 100 number-one "Praying for Time" this came out 3 September 1990.

Fast forward to current time and Listen Without Prejudice would be reissued on 20 October 2017, across a number of formats, including a 3CD+DVD super deluxe edition box set, and once again reached number one in the UK Albums Chart. Standing the test of time of 27 years after the album first topped the chart.

In fact, Listen Without Prejudice Vol. 1, which was at the top of the charts in the UK, number two in the US, and was certified 4× Platinum.

Even the titles of the songs were much deeper this time around.

The album singles were:

"Praying for Time",
"Waiting for That Day",
"Freedom! '90",
"Heal the Pain" and
"Cowboys and Angels".

Freedom (I won't let you down)
Freedom (I will not give you up)
Freedom (Gotta have some faith in the sound)

At many of his shows, George would end the concert with the song Freedom. He would say it's probably the most important word in the world today! Freedom was a smash hit and reached the No. 8 spot on the US *Billboard* Hot 100. The Singing Greek scored a top ten hit in Greece with the Greek gods smiling down. The song reminds us of Michael's prior life in Wham!, yet also introduces a new side of himself as he got a brand new face for the boys on MTV! With his new image, he is no longer too keen about the music business than he had been before. Michael didn't show himself in the video but instead starred a group of supermodels Naomi Campbell, Linda Evangelista, Tatjana Patitz, Christy Turlington, and Cindy Crawford.

Fun Facts about Freedom! 90" song and video:

A music video for the song was constantly on MTV and Vh1 playlist but George Michael doesn't actually appear in it.

Fast forward to the year 2017 and it was remastered for the documentary, *George Michael: Freedom.*

In October 2020, it premiered on YouTube in 4K for its 30th anniversary.

George Michael performed this song, alongside his single "White Light", during the closing ceremony of the 2012 London Olympics which was an amazing honor. He wore a black leather outfit along with a silver skull belt and wowed the crowd as they sang "Freeeeedom" in unison!

Linda Evangelista dyed her hair blonde right before the video

The man hanging upside down in the video was on an episode of Law & Order

It has the same director as Madonna on her "Express Yourself" music video

Battlestations with Sony

You ask too much of me
You try my patience
Your tongue, it's like a razor
You choose your words like weapons
Here we go, Battlestations

One of the most difficult times in his life was when George took to battle with Sony music who were his label owner. Even Prince supported George Michael in this case by saying that he should be able to write a ballet if he wanted. The case that George Michael filed in 1992 was completely on the merits of "Professional Slavery", he claimed that the accused, Sony, didn't properly promote his album "Listen without Prejudice" as a punishment when he turned down several recommendations. One of them was appearing in music videos which George refused to do since the album was called "Listen." Although he had made many good points against Sony such as that he should have complete creative control of his work, he eventually lost the battle but definitely not the war.

The Funky Singing Greek Won't let the Sun Go Down During Cover to Cover Tour

After the Faith tour, George was back out on the road for the "Cover to Cover Tour".

One of the best highlights of the show would be the song "Don't Let the Sun Go Down on Me", a 1991 duet with Elton John, which was also a number one hit song. The two first sang the song at the Live Aid concert in 1985 and later, George Michael's Cover to Cover tour would include the song nightly. For the final show at Wembley Arena, London in 1991, Michael brought out John as a surprise guest to sing it with him. It was an instant smash with the audience! The music video features Sir Elton John walking out on stage as George Michael announces…"Ladies and Gentleman……Mr. Elton Johhhhn!!"

The Singing Greek kept the number one vibe going following year with the song "Too Funky", for the charity project *Red Hot + Dance*; the song shot to the top of the charts in the UK and in the US. It features many amazing models and George as the director and camera man at the end.

The "Singing Greek" takes a long break from touring but goes on to release albums:

Older (which came out in 1996). was known for:

"Fastlove"

"Jesus to a Child"

These songs were all at the top of the UK charts,

The Singing Greek performed his first live shows in quite some time with a show for Radio 1 FM with just 200 audience members and an intimate show.

Unplugged Session for MTV with a little more than 500 audience members. This can be found on the Listen Without Prejudice Box Set.

Both audiences included contest winners, some of whom had traveled to London from all over the globe, as well as various VIP fans.

Patience (2004) was known for the songs:

"Amazing"

"Flawless"

"Freak"

George Michael appearing on the Oprah Winfrey show to promote the cd with his then partner Kenny Goss and explaining the LA incident to the audience. He also performed the hit song "Amazing" and as a bonus he gave Oprah Winfrey a tour of his 16th century house in Oxfordshire.

Twenty Five, in 2006, a second greatest hits album, celebrated the 25th anniversary of his music career. It was a smash number one in the UK with three new songs:

"An Easier Affair"

"Feeling Good" (cover)

"This Is Not Real Love" (a duet with Mutya Buena, then a member of the Sugababes, and now a member of Mutya Keisha Siobhan).

Chapter 6

25 Live Tour

The tour was "a celebration of George Michael's (Singing Greek's) 25-year career in music"
It promoted <u>a Greatest Hits album</u> as well as the highlights below:
It was George Michael's first tour in over 15 years! The time had finally come to tour again and the fans were thrilled to hear it!

The tour, was originally meant to have fifty dates, and would begin in Barcelona, Spain on September 23. 2006. It was scheduled to complete at Wembley Arena in London in December, however, due to popular demand from fans it continued into 2007 with more performances throughout Europe, finishing in Belfast.

One of the stops during the tour would be Athens, Greece as referred by his family the old country!

He would also be the first artist to have a concert at the new Wembley Stadium. Bonjovi was scheduled to open but was not able because of schedule conflicts.

On 25 March 2008, (Greek Independence Day) a third Leg of the 25 LIVE Tour was announced for North America. This leg included 21 dates in the United States and Canada.

This was Michael's first tour of North America in 17 years!

George Michael Back on tour and 25 Live !

Reviews for the 25 live show which kicked off in Barcelona, Spain were amazing and ticket sales were brisk selling out in minutes for the Europe legs of the tour. Some of the highlights were:

In the 25 Live tour, George Michael often dressed in all black, sporting tinted sunglasses and stubble, the look matched his sexy voice.

During the song Outside, he would dress in a police uniform to mimic the LA incident from back in the 90s.

A moving cover of Roberta Flack's "The First Time Ever I Saw Your Face",

The guitar-rocking "Faith"!

Soulful "Father Figure" backed by his amazing backup singers.

He also successfully pulled off several Wham! songs without making them sound out of date.

The set included three video screens, the middle one showing eye catching images such as snippets from the Wham! days. The other two screens depicting the show, made the concert about the music, not special effects. Pitch perfect sound made his voice crystal clear and not drowned by the music. It's not every day that a performer can create an intimate show in a large stadium with thousands of excited fans and George Michael did it! Even George stated in an interview how pleased he was with all the amazing reviews he was getting for the 25 live tour speaking from his heart!

George Michael, the Singing Greek, Takes Athens, Greece to the Edge of Heaven!

After touring much of Europe with the 25 live tour…finally, the time had come. It was his first time performing in Athens, Greece and the wait was over! For this show, expectations were high, and before the show even began, it was clear that it would be done in Singing Greek fashion. With 40,000 fans in attendance, his first tour in close to 20 years, George Michael's 25 Live Tour stopped at the OAKA stadium in Athens, Greece on an extremely hot day.

The date was July 26th 2007, and it was to be a very special night because George's family was in attendance including his father, Jack, and some very close relatives. Before the show, George's father stopped by the dressing room with another Greek singing legend, George Dalaras, to wish him luck for a great show. It was quite an honor to have him in attendance as well. During the concert, George would even speak a few words of Greek to the crowd which his aunt taught him.

At one point during the show, the Singing Greek would come out draped with the Greek Flag of blue and white and held it with pride during his hit Freedom 90. The crowd would chant his Greek name "Yorgos… Yorgos…Yorgos!!" He thanked the audience from the bottom of his heart for 25 years of being fans as the crowd erupted in applause. The sleek stage, consisted of a long, flowing screen of black tiles in the center and two LED screens on either side, the stage housed a full band and six soulful back-up singers in three-tiered cages. As fans filed in from all over Greece, that magical evening, Michael's silky voice could be heard throughout the Olympic style stadium as he sang the song "Song to the Siren." As the song ended, the crowd erupted in cheers when the Singing Greek finally entered the center stage to sing "Fast Love," ready to be in full control this magical evening!

That night, the Greek gods were smiling down as the Singing Greek masterfully, conducted the tempo of the show, entertaining the crowd like an well-seasoned popstar. He swooned effortlessly from hits like "Father Figure" and "Hard Day," Wham! classics "Everything She Wants" and "Edge of Heaven" where he had full crowd participation with the yeaa yeaa yeaa and la da de da da daa!!

He would swagger and hip-shake during hits such as "I'm Your Man" which delighted the fun filled crowd, among which were many former teen fanatics. The crowd danced and sang along for most of the show, cheering as Wham! footage and videos from the Singing Greek's solo career appeared across the screens and faded into Michael's 2000 look: salt and pepper stubble, sophisticated and amazingly sharp.

A short intermission countdown 10, 9, 8, 7, 6, 5,,,,,,,, concluded with the familiar sound of a church organ could be heard throughout the venue. Deep fan screams echoed from the top of the stadium seats down to the main floor as the Singing Greek began to sing the title track from the Faith album. It would bring back memories of the big 80s!

There were many highlights in Athens that night but one of the most beautiful was the melancholy "Jesus to a Child" and very personal love song "Amazing" - which Michael dedicated to his partner of several years, Texan entrepreneur Kenny Goss. How can one forget when he performed "Outside" (in a police uniform with fingerless gloves and tinted shades)

One of the best highlights of the show was the song "Careless Whisper" when the crowd sang along "I'm never gonna dance again" while holding and turning on the flashlights on their cellphones. Back in the day it would have been their lighters. The whole darkened arena was lit up by candlelight as George sang ….

Now that you're gone
Now that you're gone
Now that you're gone
What I did that was so wrong?

and concluded with "Freedom 90" where he had everyone raise their hands at once singing Freedom!! This show left no doubt that this modern legend transcended gender, age, and all else. Michael's spectacular show in Athens, Greece ran just under three hours, leaving every fan wanting more even if they were exhausted! It was definitely worth the 20-year wait as the Greek gods had faith it would be a great show!

Below is the set list for the Concert in Athens which George Michael performed:

25 live in Athens, Greece
"Song to the Siren" (Behind the Stage)
"Fastlove"
"Too Funky"
"Father Figure"
"Everything She Wants"
"Easier Affair"
The First time I ever Seen your Face
"Praying for Time"
"Star People"
"Flawless Go to the City"
"Shoot the Dog"

Break (John and Elvis video)
"Faith"
"Spinning the Wheel"
"Jesus to a Child"
"An Easier Affair"
"Amazing"
"I'm Your Man"
"Outside"
Encore
"Edge of Heaven"
"Careless Whisper"
"Freedom! '90"

Chapter 7

The Finals

The 25 live tour ended with two concerts at Earls Court in London named "The Final Two". Wham! fans would relate this to Wham!'s final concert at Wembley Stadium in London back in the 80s, The Final. Another final concert was later revealed. The concert was performed at Copenhagen, Denmark, and called The Final One. George Michael also toured down under with Australian concerts which were added in November 2009, with stops in Perth, Sydney, and later Melbourne in February/March 2010.

As a bonus "The Final Two", taking place in Earls Court, London on 24 and 25 August 2008 were filmed for a 25 LIVE DVD release entitled "Live in London".

At the time of his death, George Michael (*The Singing Greek*) had:
Sold over 115 million records worldwide,
Become one of the best-selling music artists of all time.
Seven number one songs on the UK Singles Chart and
Eight number one songs on the US *Billboard* Hot 100.
Two Grammy Awards,
Three Brit Awards,
Three American Music Awards,
Twelve *Billboard* Music Awards
Four MTV Video Music Awards
Six Ivor Novello Awards.
Ranked 40th on *Billboard*'s list of the Greatest Hot 100 Artists of All Time.

The Singing Greek sees a White Light in his final single while "Alive"

His final single was "White Light", and it was a commercial success, reaching number 15 on the UK Singles Chart. The song is about Michael's battle with pneumonia in late 2011, during which he almost left us for the edge of Heaven. He would sing, "Was it science that saved me, or the way that you prayed for me? Either way I thank you, I'm alive!"

The video included supermodel Kate Moss who was also a neighbor of George's in North London. She shared a memory that she and her daughter would use his swimming pool. She said: "He's got a pool, so when it's hot I'm like, 'Oh can Lila come and jump in your pool?' And he's like, 'Yeah, come over'. "And we can actually climb from garden to garden over the walls with a ladder, we've done that a couple of times." Another example of his giving heart!

George Michael (The Singing Greeks) Final Words

By many of his fans, George Michael was considered "Yorgos the Greek god" because he was so incredibly talented. In the Greek Orthodox religion, we believe in the resurrection of the dead when Jesus comes to judge the living and the dead and whose Kingdom has no end. In many of his songs, George would reference Jesus and God (ie. "Jesus to a Child") and of course we can't forget faith. Unfortunately, on October 17, 2012, George Michael performed his last ever concert which took place at Earl's Court in London. Just before he was ready to walk off the stage, George waved and spoke his last words to his audience *«Thank you London, we love you – see you soon."*

Chapter 8

*Ten things we have learned
from George Michael*

We gotta have "faith" even in the toughest times.
Remember to always "pray for time".
"Freedom" is the most important word in the world today.
No matter how difficult give it "one more try."
"Patience" is an "amazing" quality to have.
Every morning we must "Wake up to go go."
Turn a "different corner" and we may have never met.
Our love should be like "Jesus to a child."
We gotta get up to get down.
Guilty feet have got no rhythm.

Chapter 9

Favorite GM Videos

Aretha Franklin and George https://www.youtube.com/watch?v=fDxzQJaA228

George and Queen https://www.youtube.com/watch?v=46YZ8evUfKk&t=1s

George and Sir Elton John https://www.youtube.com/watch?v=RsKqMNDoR4o

George Michael Faith https://www.youtube.com/watch?v=6Cs3Pvmmv0E

George Michael in Athens https://www.youtube.com/watch?v=i4rnJv3K02Y

Wham Battle stations https://www.youtube.com/watch?v=ha2Wn51W8y4

Wham Edge of Heaven https://www.youtube.com/watch?v=cCqEyJc-wdk

Wham Careless Whisper https://www.youtube.com/watch?v=izGwDsrQ1eQ

Wham Wake Me Up Before you go go https://www.youtube.com/watch?v=pIgZ7gMze7A

Wham I'm your Man https://www.youtube.com/watch?v=6W0d9xMhZbo

George Michael in Chicago https://www.youtube.com/watch?v=-SX_E-NcCsM

George Michael in Atlanta https://www.youtube.com/watch?v=YR0-IQ56yps

George Michael in Houston https://www.youtube.com/watch?v=3uFGxOpq3Qk

George Michael With Whitney Houston https://www.youtube.com/watch?v=7EjfbyCpAxA

George Michael Fantasy https://www.youtube.com/watch?v=rWk7ykBdIA8

George Michael Freedom 90' https://www.youtube.com/watch?v=diYAc7gB-0A

George Michael and Deon Estus Heaven Help me https://www.youtube.com/watch?v=g1u_619dZ2s

Chapter 10

Epilogue

Being a fan since the big 80s, I always thought it would be fun to channel my best George Michael. Below are a few pics that were taken by my amazing friends. Many thanks to my family, friends, and the many cover bands for being so supportive because without them this book couldn't be possible. You are always in my prayers when I pray for time and I have faith that there will be more books to come. You have been there for me and I will be there for you until the end of time. Many of my friends that will read this book helped me heal the pain in order for me to soar to the edge of heaven. Writing this book has been a learning experience and I am sure that I will give it one more try. Turn a different corner and we may have never met.

About the Author

George who is also of Greek descent from the island of Chios, Greece, has been a fan since his high school years in the 80s. He has seen George Michael in concert several times. Once during the Cover to Cover tour and 25 Live tour in 2008. Both were a religious music experience for him. People are always surprised that his name is George and that he is Greek too. He has authored cookbooks such as "The Lighter Side of Dark Chocolate: Take it to Heart." He enjoys attending totally tubular events such as the "Back to the 80s fest" in Frankenmuth every year.

Printed in the United States
by Baker & Taylor Publisher Services